SPARK LAW SERIES®

LABOR LAW

McLaren Legal Publishers LLC
New York

ALSO AVAILABLE IN THIS SERIES:

Agency & Partnership
Antitrust
Bankruptcy
Civil Procedure
Family Law
Federal Income Tax
Labor Law
Wills & Trusts

SPARK LAW SERIES®

LABOR LAW

First Edition

Denise Esmerado, Esq.
Seton Hall Law School

ISBN 10: 0-9801482-6-X
ISBN 13: 978-0-9801482-6-8

Published by
McLaren Legal Publishers LLC
136 West 21st Street, 8th Floor
New York, NY 10011

Web: www.mclarenpublishing.com
Email: contact@mclarenpublishing.com

Printed in the United States of America

HOW TO USE THIS BOOK

This law school study aid is a non-keyed book. While it includes many of the key critical cases in the subject addressed, it is meant to provide an overall rigorous review of the topic indicated and convey key concepts and points of law for general study. For a keyed book linked to a specific casebook, please use our Legal Path Series® of keyed books.

"All of what you need, none of what you don't"

Our law school study guides give you exactly what you need to understand the key principles of the subject, including the sometimes elusive Black Letter law. We are not a replacement for an in depth legal analysis of the subject matter covered; however, we do present what is absolutely critical in a very concise format.

"Notes"

We have included a number of pages which were intentionally left blank so that you may take notes on them. This section is entitled "NOTES" and comprises the last half of the book. We did this purposely so that you may consolidate all of your information for class/exam prep in one place without having to reference a number of sources by jumping from book-to-book-to-notebook-to-laptop. We felt this was especially important for those of you who may be taking an open-book exam in this upper level course or are studying for the Bar Exam.

Abbreviations used in this book

Use of the word "his" in this book is gender neutral and encompasses both "his" and "her."

TABLE OF CONTENTS

Labor Law
SPARK LAW SERIES

I. EMPLOYMENT AT WILL

An employment relationship for no specific duration is presumed in most states to be an employment relationship "at will". That is, the relationship can be terminated "at the will" of either party; the employer or the employee. Technically, either the employer or the employee can terminate the employment relationship with or without notice and without consequence. As such, the employee is not guaranteed a job for any specific duration; he or she does not necessarily have job security. The employer can terminate the relationship at any time or the employee can quit at any time.

However, despite an at-will relationship, an employer cannot terminate an employee in violation of law such as for discriminatory reasons; based on the employee's age, disability, sex, race, color, religion or national origin. There are federal statutes that protect an employee from termination or other adverse employment action, such as demotion, failing to promote an employee or providing disproportionate compensation and benefits. The statutes that guard against discriminatory actions with certain protected classifications of persons are Title VII of the Civil Rights Act of 1964, the Americans with Disabilities Act, the Age Discrimination in Employment Act and the Equal Pay Act, an amendment to the Fair Labor Standard's Act.

This book will discuss these statutes as well as the Federal Family and Medical Leave Act, which allows an employee to take leave from work without having to be concerned about job security and termination.

Finally, this book will also discuss the Fair Labor Standards Act, which deals with child labor laws, minimum wage, overtime pay and record keeping requirements for workers.

Labor Law
SPARK LAW SERIES

II. TITLE VII OF THE CIVIL RIGHTS ACT OF 1964

A. What is Title VII of the Civil Rights Act of 1964?

Title VII of the Civil Rights Act of 1964 is considered the focus of employment discrimination law because it prohibits discrimination based on race, color, religion, sex (including pregnancy) and national origin.[1] It does not include the protected classifications of age or disability. The Age Discrimination in Employment Act (ADEA) and the Americans with Disabilities Act (ADA) prohibit discrimination based upon such characteristics. Title VII applies to employers, labor organizations and employment agencies.

In order to make a claim for discrimination under Title VII, the aggrieved employee must initially process his or her claim through the Equal Employment Opportunity Commission (EEOC). The EEOC investigates the charges, and where there is reasonable cause to believe that a violation has occurred, it attempts to resolve the complaint informally.[2] If conciliation fails, the EEOC has the power to file suit. If the EEOC elects not to file suit, the charging party may obtain a "right to sue" letter. This letter allows the charging party to file his/her claim in court within 90 days of receiving the right to sue letter.

---

[1] 42 U.S.C. 2000e et seq.
[2] 42 U.S.C. 2000e-5(b).

B. Who Qualifies as an Employer Under Title VII?

Pursuant to the statute, "employer" has a two part definition:

(1) A person in industry affecting commerce. Person includes legal entity. Any person with requisite number of employees will somehow affect commerce.

(2) Employer has at least fifteen (15) employees. In order the count against the fifteen (15) employee threshold, the employee must be employed for each working day for twenty (20) or more calendar weeks in the current or previous year. The weeks need not be consecutive. Therefore, part-time and casual employees do not count, but such workers are protected by Title VII. That is, such employees may allege violation of Title VII and claim discrimination.

C. How are the Protected Classifications Defined?

a. Race and Color

Title VII prohibits discrimination based on a person's racial origins or based upon the color of a person's skin. It prohibits discrimination because of the race of a spouse of the applicant or employee. For example, a Caucasian male applicant is invited back by a potential employer for a second interview. After the interview is scheduled but before it takes place, the applicant voluntarily discloses that his wife is African-American. Potential employer informs applicant that it is no longer interested in hiring applicant for the position sought.

b. Religion

The statute prohibits discrimination because of one's religion, unless religion is a bona fide occupational qualification. For example, Jewish male wishes to be considered for the position of a minister to lead a Christian congregation. Being of the

Christian faith can be considered a bona fide occupational qualification for the position of minister.

"Religion" includes established and organized faiths such as Baptists, Catholic, Judaism or Islam as well as unconventional faiths with sincerely held beliefs.

> Moral or ethical beliefs as to what is right and wrong which are sincerely held with the strength of traditional religious views. . . . The fact that no religious group espouses such beliefs or the fact that a religion to which the individual professes to belong may not accept such belief, will not determine whether the belief is a religious belief of the employee or prospective employee. [3]

Title VII also protects atheists from discrimination based on the absence of religious belief, as well as discrimination for activity that conflicts with the employee's religious belief. For example, an employee may claim violation of Title VII if the employee can establish that he/she was discharged because the employer disapproved of his/her atheistic views.

D. How Does an Employee/Applicant Establish that the Employer Failed to Accommodate His/Her Religion?

In order to establish a prima facie case of religious discrimination based on failure to accommodate an employee's religious beliefs, the aggrieved employee (or applicant) must prove the following elements:

(1) The religious practice is sincerely held;

---

[3] 29 C.F.R. 1605.1.

(2) The employee informed the employer of the conflict between the practice and the employee's job obligations; and,

(3) The employee was subjected to discriminatory treatment for complying with the practice.

The employer then has the opportunity to demonstrate that it is unable to reasonably accommodate the employee's religious observance or practice without undue hardship on the employer's business.[4]

In situations where an accommodation would impose an undue hardship, no accommodation is required. For example, a sales associate is unable to work on Saturday in observance of the Sabbath. The employer needs two sales associates for its retail department store to work on Saturday, the busiest shopping day of the week for the employer. The employer can refuse to allow the employee to be off every Saturday as it would cause undue hardship to the employer's business.

a. National Origin

"National origin" discrimination occurs when discriminatory practices are based on the place in which one's ancestor's lived.[5] It includes all distinct cultural heritages or geographical origins even if no current nation exists. As such, discrimination against Armenians, Cajuns or Gypsies can be national origin discrimination.[6] Discrimination against those who speak English with a foreign accent can be national original discrimination.[7] However, an employer may require employees to be able to communicate in English if the employer has a legitimate business reason for the requirement. Such a requirement based on a legitimate business reason is not in and of itself national origin discrimination.

---

[4] 42 U.S.C. 2000e(j).
[5] Dawavendewa v. Salt River Project Agric. Improvement & Power Distr., 154 F.3d 1117 (9th Cir. 1998).
[6] Pejic v. Hughes Helicopters, 840 F.2d 667(9th Cir. 1988).
[7] Berke v. Ohio Department of Public Welfare, 628 F.2d 980(6th Cir. 1980).

b. Sex

"Sex" as a protected classification is defined very specifically under Title VII. Title VII states that "[t]he terms 'because of sex' or 'on the basis of sex' include, but are not limited to, because of or on the basis of pregnancy, childbirth, or related medical conditions; and women affected by pregnancy, childbirth, or related medical conditions shall be treated the same for all employment related purposes…".[8] It is construed narrowly to refer to gender not to affectional or sexual preferences.[9] Moreover, men are protected against sex discrimination under the same standards that apply to women. For example, a hospital cannot refuse to hire a male as a nurse because the nursing professional has traditionally been a female-dominant field. An employer cannot demand levels of performance or standards of conduct for members of one gender that are not required of another gender. A rule that only applies to one gender is considered sex discrimination. Employers may not measure performance in terms of sexual stereotyping related to proper roles and behavior of genders. For example, a law firm may not refuse to promote a female to partner because she does not wear make-up, a stereotypical expectation of women.[10]

c. Sexual Harassment

Title VII also recognizes a cause of action for sexual harassment or harassment based upon any protected classification in addition to sex. The EEOC defines sexual harassment as:

---

[8] 42 U.S.C. 2000e(k).

[9] Smith v. Liberty Mutual Insurance Co., 569 F.2d 325 (5th Cir. 1978).

[10] See, Price Waterhouse v. Hopkins,490 U.S. 228 (1989) Court determined that the employer's refusal to offer a partnership to a female associate was sex discrimination because it measured the plaintiff's performance against stereotyped expectations of female behavior. Specifically, the plaintiff was described as "macho", "over compensated for being a woman", "a lady using foul language". The employer advised the employee to "walk more femininely, wear makeup, have her hair styled and wear jewelry" in order to improve her chances for promotion.

Unwelcome sexual advances, requests for sexual favors, and other verbal or physical conduct of a sexual nature constitutes sexual harassment when:

- submission of such conduct is made either explicitly or implicitly a term or condition of an individual's employment; or

- submission to or rejection of such conduct by an individual is used as the basis for employment decisions affecting such individual; or

- such conduct has the purpose or effect of unreasonably interfering with an individual's work performance or creating an intimidating, hostile or offensive working environment.

There are two (2) types of sexual harassment: quid pro quo and hostile work environment harassment. Quid pro quo harassment occurs when "submission of such conduct is made either explicitly or implicitly a term or condition of an individual's employment or submission to or rejection of such conduct by an individual is used as the basis for employment decisions affecting such individual" as provided above. For example, male supervisor requests that female employee share a room with him at hotel for overnight meeting and remarks that he will determine whether the female employee will get a raise in salary after returning from the trip.

Hostile work environment harassment occurs when "conduct has the purpose or effect of unreasonably interfering with an individual's work performance or creating an intimidating, hostile or offensive working environment", as explained above. For example, comments about an employee's clothing, attractiveness or desire to engage in sexual relations with the employee can give rise to hostile work environment sexual harassment claim.

Same sex harassment can support a claim under Title VII in that an employee may be sexually harassed by another employee of the same sex.

d. Pregnancy

Title VII defines "sex" to include "pregnancy, child birth and related conditions."[11] The statute also provides that "[w]omen affected by pregnancy, child birth or related medical conditions shall be treated the same for all employment-related purposes, including receipt of benefits under fringe benefit programs as other persons not so affected but similar in their ability or inability to work. . . ."[12] An employer may not reject a woman because of her gender or because she is pregnant. For example, an employer extends an offer of employment to a female applicant for the position of receptionist. Pursuant to company policy, the employee is subject to a medical examination. The results of the exam reveal that the woman is pregnant. The company can not retract the offer of employment because it learned that the woman is pregnant.[13]

e. Sexuality and Homosexuality

Title VII does not recognize discrimination on the basis of sexual orientation or sexual preference while many state laws do. Therefore, under Title VII it is not sex discrimination to discriminate against persons who are perceived to be homosexual, transsexual or bi-sexual. Hence it is not actionable under Title VII to discriminate against a male who cross dresses or is effeminate.[14] Moreover, similar issues such as transvestitism

---

[11] 42 U.S.C. 2000e(k).

[12] 42 U.S.C. 2000e(k).

[13] The Federal Pregnancy Discrimination Act of 1978 prohibits discrimination on the basis of pregnancy such as terms of medical benefit programs, disability programs, health insurance or other leave plans. Pregnancy is to be treated like any other disability in this regard.

[14] Smith v. Liberty Mutual Insurance Co., 569 F.2d 325 (5th Cir. 1978); Powell v. Read's, Inc., 436 F.Supp. 369 (D.C. Ma. 1977).

and transsexualism are not considered handicaps. The Americans with Disabilities Act (ADA) excludes from the definition of protected disabilities, homosexuality, transvestitism and transsexualism.

E. What are the Theories of Liability?

There are two (2) theories of liability under Title VII: disparate impact and disparate treatment.

Disparate impact is when a selection system has an unjustified adverse affect on a protected class of persons. For example, company has a policy that it will only hire employees from Jonesville College. Jonesville's student body is predominantly Caucasian. The employer's selection process has an unjustified effect or adverse impact on racial minority applicants.

The other theory of liability, disparate treatment, occurs when discrimination is imposed on a person or persons because of his or her protected classification. The person can establish discrimination based upon direct evidence or circumstantial evidence. If the employee has direct evidence of the employer's discriminatory motivation, such as written or oral statements, the burden then shifts to the employer to establish that the same decision regarding the employee would have been made for legitimate reasons. For example, a terminated female employee makes a claim of discrimination pursuant to Title VII based upon her sex. She bases her claim on an e-mail from the company's president to the employee's supervisor stating that the president wants to terminate the employee because he believes that the position should be staffed by a male. The employer defends that the employee would have been terminated anyway because over the past year the employee has been chronically late to work.

F. What Kind of Damages are Available to an Aggrieved Employee Under Title VII?

a. Reinstatement

For an employee or applicant who experiences adverse employment action for example, is discharged, not promoted or not hired, he/she may be reinstated to the position he/she had before termination or sought as a promotion or new hire and not granted. However reinstatement may not be an appropriate remedy if no position is available; when a working relationship between the parties would be antagonistic; or, the employer has a longstanding resistance to discrimination efforts.[15]

b. Front Pay

As an alternative to reinstatement, the employee may be awarded front pay. Front pay is a calculation of future lost wages to place the employee as near as possible to the situation he/she would be in if the wrong had not been committed. Front pay can be difficult to evaluate given that intervening factors may affect the employee's future employability, such as the employee's life expectancy, the likelihood of him or her being terminated for valid business reasons and the employee's diligence in securing alternate employment to mitigate his or her damages.

---

[15] Finlay v. United States Postal Service, EEOC Appeal No. 01942985 (April 29, 1997).

c. Back Pay

Back pay is defined as the wages and benefits the aggrieved employee would have received if not for the discrimination. It includes the value of fringe benefits, raises and cost of living adjustments. It is generally calculated from when the employee would have received the position he sought or would be in but for his termination, up to reinstatement (or alternatively front pay).

d. Compensatory Damages

In addition to back pay, an aggrieved employee may also receive compensatory damages; damages designed to make the employee "whole", such as compensation for emotional distress, loss of enjoyment of life and other non-pecuniary losses.

e. Punitive Damages

Punitive damages are intended to punish the wrongdoer for its conduct and deter it from engaging in such conduct in the future. Punitive damages cannot be collected against a governmental employer. In order to receive punitive damages against the employer, the aggrieved employee must establish that the employer engaged in discriminatory practices with malice or with reckless indifference to the protected rights of the employee. Punitive damages may be granted according to a sliding scale (for a combined total of punitive and compensatory damages) based upon the size of the employer. For employers who employ between fifteen (15) to 100 employees, damages are capped at $50,000.00; 101-200 employees, recovery allows for a maximum of $100,000; 201-500, the award is limited to $200,000; more than 500, there is a maximum award of $300,000.[16]

---

[16] 42 U.S.C. 1981a(b)(3).

f.   Attorneys' Fees

Attorneys' fees can be awarded to the prevailing employee in a Title VII claim. Attorneys' fees can also be awarded to a prevailing employer, but it is rarely granted to a prevailing employer unless the employer can establish that the claims made by the employee under Title VII were frivolous or groundless.[17]

g.   Liquidated Damages

Title VII does not permit an employee to recover liquidated damages. Liquidated damages allows for a double recovery of damages for example, a double recovery for lost wages. However, liquidated damages under Title VII are not available to an employee for lost wages or otherwise.

---

[17] Parker v. Sony Pictures Entertainment, 260 F.3d 100 (2d Cir. 2001).

Labor Law
SPARK LAW SERIES

III. AMERICANS WITH DISABILITIES ACT (ADA)

A. What Is the Americans With Disabilities Act?

The Americans with Disabilities Act (ADA) went into effect on July 26, 1990. It is designed to eliminate discrimination against individuals with disabilities in society. Disabilities include both physical and mental impairments. Since disability discrimination can occur in a number of contexts, Congress adopted the ADA with separate titles. These areas primarily concern employment (Title I); public services (Title II); public accommodations (Title III); and telecommunications (Title IV).   This chapter will focus on disability discrimination pursuant to Title I.

Like Title VII and the Age Discrimination in Employment Act (ADEA), in order to make a claim for discrimination under the ADA, the aggrieved employee must initially process his or her claim through the Equal Employment Opportunity Commission (EEOC).   The EEOC investigates the charges, and where there is reasonable cause to believe that a violation has occurred, it attempts to resolve the complaint informally.[18] If conciliation fails, the EEOC has the power to file suit. If the EEOC elects not to file suit, the charging party may obtain a "right to sue" letter. This letter allows the charging party to file his/her claim in court within 90 days of receiving the right to sue letter.

B. What are some of the Important Definitions under the ADA?

Situations involving violations of the ADA can be very fact-sensitive. The viability of an ADA claim can depend on whether the claimant fulfills the definitions under the statute. The definitions of disability and major life activity are two important terms under the ADA.

"Disability" is defined in the ADA as a physical or mental impairment that substantially limits one or more of the major life activities of such

---

[18] 29 C.F.R. 1601.1 et seq.

individual; the individual has a record of such impairment; or, the individual is regarded as having such impairment.[19]

"Major life activities" are those basic activities that the average person in the general population can perform with little or no difficulty. These activities include caring for oneself, performing menial tasks, walking, seeing, breathing, learning, and working.[20]

To determine whether an individual is disabled under the ADA, consideration should first be given to whether the person has a physical or mental impairment. An impairment that prevents an individual from performing a major life activity substantially limits that major life activity.

In determining whether a major life activity is substantially limited, the following factors are evaluated:

(1)   nature and severity of the impairment;
(2)   duration or expected duration of the impairment;
(3)   permanent or long term impact, or the expected permanent or long term impact of or resulting from the impairment.[21]

An individual who is not substantially limited with respect to any major life activity may be substantially limited with respect to working.

An individual who is unable to perform one particular job may be able to perform other common jobs, and therefore not considered substantially limited in the performance of working. In order to establish that the employee is substantially limited in the major life activity of working, the employee must demonstrate that he or she cannot work in a broad class of jobs.[22] For example, an employee who is blind in one eye and therefore unable to obtain a commercial driver's license and drive a commercial vehicle may not be impeded in performing most other jobs.

Limitation on the major life activity must be substantial. This precludes impairments that interfere in only a minor way with the performance of manual tasks from qualifying as disabilities. The major life activities must be

---

[19] 42 U.S.C. 12102(2).
[20] 45 C.F.R. 84.3(j)(2)(ii); 29 C.F.R. 1630.2(j).
[21] 29 C.F.R. 1630.2(j).
[22] Sutton v. United Air Lines, Inc., 527 U.S. 471 (1999).

those activities that are of central importance to daily life. Such a determination is done on a case by case basis.[23] For example, an employee claims to be disabled with carpal tunnel syndrome from performing on an automobile assembly line. The employee can not engage in repetitive work with her hands and arms extended at or above her shoulders for long periods of time. However the employee can carry out her household chores, bath, brush her teeth and the like. The employee may not be limited in a major life activity as she could perform a variety of tasks central to most peoples' lives and is simply limited in performing the tasks associated with her job.

The ADA not only protects individuals who have or had impairment; it also protects those perceived to be impaired. For example, an employee wrongfully believed to have cancer and treated discriminatorily is protected under the ADA.[24]

Temporary non-chronic impairments of short duration with little or no long-term or permanent impact are usually not disabilities. For example, broken limbs, concussion, sprained joint, appendicitis and influenza.[25]

Some conditions that can be controlled, such as through medication, may not be considered a disability such as diabetes, high blood pressure or asthma.

Pregnancy is specifically excluded under the ADA. Yet, complications from pregnancy and childbirth might be covered depending upon the specific circumstances of the condition. For example, a woman who develops uncontrollable diabetes as a result of being pregnant can have a protected disability under the ADA.[26]

---

[23] Toyota Motor Manufacturing v. Williams, 534 U.S. 184 (2002)
[24] 28 C.F.R. 36.104; 29 C.F.R. 1630.2(h)(1) and (2).
[25] 42 U.S.C. 12102(2).
[26] Id.

C. What are the Specifics of Title I as it Applies in an Employment Context?

Title I focuses on employment. However, not all employers are covered by the ADA. The ADA applies only to employers that are covered entities.

"Employer" is defined as a person engaged in an industry affecting commerce who has fifteen (15) or more employees for each working day in each of 20 or more calendar weeks".[27] Many employers are excluded from the ADA including: the United States or a corporation wholly owned by the government, Indian tribes and a bona fide private membership clubs.

"Covered entities" is defined as employers, employment agencies, labor organizations and joint labor management committees.

Covered employers are prohibited from discriminating against a "qualified individual with a disability" as to job applications, hiring, advancement, discharge, compensation training or other terms and conditions of employment.

A qualified individual with a disability is defined as an individual with a disability who with or without reasonable accommodation can perform the essential functions of the employment position that such individual holds or desires.[28] This requirement contains a number of terms that must be defined in order to understand an employer's obligation as it relates to an individual with a disability.

D. What are the Essential Functions of a Position?

Essential functions of a position are defined as the primary job duties that are intrinsic to the employment position the individual holds or desires. It does not include marginal or peripheral functions that are incidental to the performance of primary job functions. If an employer has prepared a written

---

[27] Although the ADA affects only those employers with fifteen (15) or more employees, many state statutes that prohibit discrimination based upon disability have minimum employee threshold requirements for applicability.

[28] 42 U.S.C. 12131(2).

description for advertising or interviewing applicants for a position, the description is often considered strong evidence of the essential functions of the job. Job functions can be essential because of the limited number of employees available to perform the task or the responsibilities may be highly specialized. For example, a clerk typist, who primarily types but is also responsible for occasional filing and answering telephones, may not be able to perform the essential functions of her position if carpal tunnel syndrome prevents her from typing. However, if the employee can type and answer the telephone, but is unable to properly file documents like she once did due to a mental disability, it could be determined that the employee can perform the essential functions of her position. The occasional filing responsibilities of the job are peripheral to the major responsibility of the position, typing.

E. What are Reasonable Accommodations?

An employer is required to provide a reasonable accommodation to qualified disabled individuals. Such an accommodation may include:

(1)   making existing facilities readily accessible and usable;
(2)   job restructuring;
(3)   modification to work schedules, equipment or devices;
(4)   providing qualified interpreters or readers;
(5)   reassignment to vacant positions. [29]

This is not an exhaustive list of reasonable accommodations. The employer is expected to engage in an interactive process with the employee to determine what would be a reasonable accommodation in connection with the employee's disability.

Reasonable accommodations may require employers to spend money to assist the disabled employee in carrying out his/her job responsibilities. However, the requirement to make reasonable accommodations is not limitless. The ADA takes into account whether the accommodation is an "undue hardship" on the employer in that the action will be a significant difficulty or expense to the employer. For example, an employer may be required to accommodate an employee's hearing impediment by providing an

---

[29] 42 U.S.C. 12111(9); 29 C.F.R. 1630.2(o).

acoustic enhancement device for the employee's telephone, at the employer's expense.

F. How Can an Employer Establish that the Accommodation Will Create an Undue Hardship?

The following factors are considered in determining whether an accommodation would present an undue hardship to the employer.

(1) The nature and cost of the accommodation requested under the ADA;

(2) The overall financial resources of the facility, including the number of persons employed at the facility, the effect on expenses and resources, the impact on the operation of the facility;

(3) The number, type and location of related facilities;

(4) The composition, structure, and functions of the workplace; and,

(5) The geographic separateness, administrative or fiscal relationship of a related facility or facilities to the specific entity that employs the employee. [30]

G. What is an Employer's Obligation Concerning Accommodation with Light-Duty and Temporary Positions?

Many employers offer light duty positions to employees who are recovering from injuries that they incur on the job until the employees can work to full capacity. Light duty positions usually are more sedentary or less physically demanding in comparison to the work an employee usually performs.

Employers are not permitted to reserve these positions for employees who incur work related injuries when an employee may require a light-duty

---

[30] 29 C.F.R. 1630.2(p).

position based upon an ADA disability. However, employers are not required to create light-duty positions as an accommodation. Nevertheless light-duty positions are usually of a temporary nature. If such is the case the employer can offer a disabled employee the light-duty position as an accommodation on a temporary basis. However if the employer plans on removing a permanently disabled employee from a temporary light-duty position, the employer should consider other accommodations for the employee upon removal.[31]

H. What if an Employee's Disability Causes Him/Her to be Excessively Absent, Does the Employer Have an Obligation to Accommodate the Employee's Excessive Absenteeism?

If the employee's absence prevents the employee from performing the essential functions of his/her job, the employer can claim that the employee's absence is causing an undue hardship on the employer.

For example, if an employee's asthma triggered by cigarette smoke causes her to be excessively absent, the employer may be justified in denying the employee leave when her disability prevents her from working. The employer may claim that the employee is essentially requesting not to perform her job in that the employee requests an accommodation which defeats her ability to perform a function of her job, namely, attendance. The employer may allege that regular attendance is regarded as an essential function of the employee's position.[32] The employer may further claim that such an accommodation would impose an undue hardship on the employer's operations. Specifically, when the employee is absent without prior notice the employee's department can not function normally. Having another employee continuously perform the employee's job responsibilities is burdensome.[33]

---

[31] See, EEOC :Guidance on Workers' Compensation and ADA , issued by the ADA division of the EEOC's Office of Legal Counsel, September 3, 1996 as provided by The Bureau of National Affairs, Inc. (1996).

[32] EEOC v. Yellow Freight System, Inc., 253 F.3d 943 (7th Cir. 2001)..

[33] Hendry v. GTE North, Inc., 896 F.Supp. 816 (D.C. 1995).

I. What Defenses May an Employer Allege When Charged with Discriminating Against an Employee Based Upon His/Her Disability?

An employer can defend that a reasonable accommodation to the employee's job cannot be provided. Not only can an employer claim that the employee's excessive absenteeism, albeit related to the employee's disability, cannot be accommodated, but it can also claim that the accommodation simply cannot be provided based upon the nature of the employer's business. For example, an employee works at a power plant. The facility is designed with safety in mind, properly storing and maintaining dangerous substances. The employee, whose disability has recently required him to rely on a wheelchair, can no longer physically carry out his job responsibilities of insuring that the substances are being stored at safe temperatures within the plant. The employer may allege that it can not redesign the facility to allow the employee access to the product storage areas by wheelchair without compromising the safe maintenance of the materials. That is, the accommodation required of the employee cannot be provided.

An employer may also claim that the individual's disability poses a direct threat to the health or safety of him/herself or other individuals in the work place. "Direct threat" is defined as a significant risk to the health or safety of others that cannot be eliminated by reasonable accommodation. [34] For example, a security officer for a university is required to patrol the campus equipped with a firearm. The employee has a recurrent dream that he pulled his revolver from his holster and pointed it at his supervisor and is under the care of a psychotherapist. The employee could be said to be a direct threat to his supervisor or others based upon his state of mind. [35]

---

[34] 42 U.S.C. 12111(3).
[35] Layser v. Morrison, 935 F. Supp. 562 (E.D. Pa. 1995).

J. Do Employers Have an Obligation to Inform Employees of Their Rights Under the ADA?

All covered entities under Title I are required to post notices in an accessible format to applicants, employees and others describing the provision of the ADA.

K. What are the Theories of Liability for an ADA Claim?

Like Title VII there are two (2) theories of liability under the ADA: disparate impact and disparate treatment. Disparate impact is when a selection system has an unjustified adverse affect on a protected class of persons, in this case disabled persons. For example, a company requires that as part of the selection process for all potential employees, the candidates must fill out a written application. Potential employees who are blind can claim that this requirement has a disparate impact on them in that they are precluded from seeking employment at the company because they cannot write out their application. The company may be required to accommodate blind applicants with the application process by providing a representative of the company to transcribe the information requested for a blind candidate.

The other theory of liability, disparate treatment, occurs under the ADA when discrimination is imposed on a person or persons because of his or her disability. The person can establish discrimination based upon direct evidence or circumstantial evidence. If the employee has direct evidence of the employer's discriminatory motivation, such as written or oral statements, the burden then shift to the employer to establish that the same decision regarding the employee would have been made for legitimate reasons. For example, terminated employee makes a claim of discrimination against her employer pursuant to the ADA based upon her disability. She bases her claim on an e-mail from the company's president to the employee's supervisor stating that the president wants to terminate the employee because he believes that she is costing the company too much in healthcare costs due to her disability. The employer defends that the employee would have been terminated anyway because last month she gave the president inaccurate information regarding a project for one of the company's largest customers, which cost the company thousands of dollars.

Additionally, an employee can also make a claim of failure to accommodate based upon disability, similar to a claim of failure to accommodate based upon religion under Title VII, however, there are two schools of thought as to who has the burden in establishing that an accommodation is reasonable. One theory provides that the employee must establish that he has a defined disability and is qualified. If he needs an accommodation, he must identify the accommodation and establish its general reasonableness. [36] The second theory provides that the employee present some evidence that he can perform the essential functions of his position with some accommodation. The employer then has the opportunity to establish that no reasonable accommodation is possible. [37]

L. What Damages are Available to an Aggrieved Employee Under the ADA?

The ADA adopted the same remedial provisions of Title VII.

a. Reinstatement

Like Title VII, reinstatement is available under the ADA for an employee who is discharged, not promoted or not hired based upon his/her disability. The employee may be reinstated to the position he or she had before termination or sought as a promotion or as a new hire and not granted. Reinstatement is often not a suitable remedy when the relationship between the employee and the employer is so strained as a result of the disability discrimination claim that imposing an employer/employee relationship would be inappropriate. It also may not be appropriate if no positions are available or if the employer has a longstanding resistance to discrimination efforts. [38]

---

[36] Stewart v. Happy Herman's Cheshire Bridge Inc., 117 F.3d 1278 (11th Cir. 1997).
[37] Benson v. Northwest Airlines , 62 F.3d 1108 (8th Cir. 1995).
[38] Finlay v. United States Postal Service, supra.

b. Front Pay

Under the ADA, like Title VII, an alternative to reinstatement is the award of front pay. Front pay is a calculation of future lost wages. Front pay can be difficult to evaluate given intervening factors that can influence an employee's future wages. Such intervening factors can be the employee's life expectancy, the likelihood of him being terminated for valid business reasons and the employee's diligence in securing alternate employment to mitigate his damages.

c. Back Pay

Back pay is defined as the wages and benefits the aggrieved employee would have received if not for the discrimination. It includes the value of fringe benefits, raises and cost of living adjustments. The employee may also receive interest on the back pay. It is generally calculated from when the employee would have received the position sought up to reinstatement or front pay.

d. Compensatory Damages

Under the ADA, in addition to back pay, an aggrieved employee may also receive compensatory damages, damages designed to make the employee "whole", such as compensation for emotional distress, loss of enjoyment of life and other non-pecuniary losses.

e. Punitive Damages

Punitive damages are available under the ADA. Punitive damages are intended to punish the wrongdoer for its conduct and deter it from engaging in such conduct in the future. Punitive damages cannot be collected against a governmental employer. The aggrieved employee must establish that the employer engaged in discriminatory practices with malice or with reckless indifference to the protected rights of the employee. Like Title VII, punitive damages may be granted to an employee according to a sliding scale (for a combined total of compensatory and punitive damages) based upon the size of the employer. For employers who employ between fifteen (15) to 100 employees, damages are capped out at $50,000.00; 101-200 employees, recovery allows at a maximum of $100,000; 201-500, the cap is $200,000; more than 500, there is a maximum amount of $300,000 in recovery of punitive damages.[39]

f. Attorneys' Fees

Attorneys' fees can be awarded to the prevailing employee in an ADA claim. Attorneys' fees can also be awarded to a prevailing employer, but it is rarely granted to a prevailing employer unless the employer can establish that the claims made by the employee under the ADA were frivolous or groundless.[40]

g. Liquidated Damages

The ADA does not permit an employee to recover liquidated damages. Liquidated damages allows for a double recovery of damages for example, a double recovery for lost wages. However, liquidated damages are not available for lost wages or any other claim for damages under the ADA.

---

[39] 42 U.S.C. 1981(a)-(b)(3).
[40] Buchhannon Bd. & Care Home, Inc. v. W.Va. Dept. of Health, 532 U.S. 598 (2001); Parker v. Sony Pictures Entertainment, 260 F.3d 100 (2d Cir. 2001).

IV. AGE DISCRIMINATION IN EMPLOYMENT ACT OF 1967

A. <u>What is the Age Discrimination in Employment Act?</u>

The Age Discrimination in Employment Act (ADEA) prohibits discrimination against individuals who are 40 years old or older.[41]

The ADEA, like Title VII and the ADA, reaches all aspects of work place discrimination such as hiring, assignments, promotions, environment and discharge.

It prohibits an employer from imposing on workers of one age group conditions of employment that are not imposed on other age classes. Standards of performance and discipline must be applied equally to all age groups.[42] For example, an employer cannot require employees over the age of 50 to submit to a physical exam and not require workers under age 50 to do the same.

Like Title VII and the ADA, in order to make a claim for discrimination under the ADEA, the aggrieved employee must initially process his or her claim through the Equal Employment Opportunity Commission (EEOC). The EEOC investigates the charges, and where there is reasonable cause to believe that a violation has occurred, it attempts to resolve the complaint informally.[43] If conciliation fails, the EEOC has the power to file suit. If the EEOC elects not to file suit, the charging party may obtain a "right to sue" letter. This letter allows the charging party to file his/her claim in court within 90 days of receiving the right to sue letter.

---

[41] 29 U.S.C. 621 et seq.
[42] <u>Shager v. Upjohn Company,</u> 913 F.2d 398 (7th Cir. 1990).
[43] 42 U.S.C. 2000e-5(b).

B. Which Employers are Subject the ADEA?

The ADEA covers employers with 20 or more employees engaged in an industry affecting interstate commerce that has 20 or more employees for each working day in each of 20 or more calendar weeks in the current or preceding calendar year. It covers employment agencies as well as labor organizations.[44]

C. What are the Elements of a Claim of Age Discrimination Pursuant to the ADEA?

In order to establish a violation of the ADEA, the aggrieved employee (or applicant) must establish:

(1)   The employee is in an age protected class (age 40 or older);

(2)   The employee was qualified for the position he sought, or was performing his job satisfactorily;

(3)   He was nevertheless not promoted to the position he sought or was terminated from the position he held; and,

(4)   The successful candidate who was promoted or hired was outside of the employee's age protected class or the employee was replaced by someone outside his protected class.[45]

The employer has the opportunity to present a legitimate non-discriminatory reason for the adverse action taken against the aggrieved employee.[46] If the employer presents a legitimate non-discriminatory reason

---

[44] 29 U.S.C. 630.

[45] Lawrence v. National Westminster Bank of New Jersey, 98 F. 3d 61(3d Cir. 1996).

[46] Id.

for its actions, the employee then must has the opportunity to establish that the employer's decision was a pretext or "cover up" for age discrimination.[47]

D. When Can an Employer's Reason for Taking Adverse Employment Action Against the Employee Not Violate the ADEA?

Employers may take "any action otherwise prohibited . . . where the differentiation is based on reasonable factors other than age."[48] Reasonable factors other than age include credentials such as education, prior experience, and systems that measure merit or the quality or quantity of performance. As long as performance standards are uniformly applied, persons who do not measure up to those standards may be discharged "for good cause" regardless of their age, or may be justified as not being the best candidate for a position in terms of hiring or promotion.[49]

E. Can a Layoff Violate the ADEA?

A reduction in force or layoff situation violates the ADEA if it was prompted by a desire to eliminate older workers within an age group.[50] For example, an employer wants to bring in a younger sales force to change the image of the company. The employer lays off a number of sales employees who all are over 50. The layoff does not affect any sales employees who are under 40. However, the layoff can violate the ADEA because it was motivated by the age of its sales force.

Reductions in force prompted by economic conditions, which resulted in all workers being laid off, regardless of age, does not necessarily create a prima facie case of age discrimination.[51] For example, a company is losing money. It decides to lay off all of its vice presidents to save money. The layoff affects all vice president positions regardless of age.

---

[47] Id.

[48] 29 U.S.C. 623.

[49] See, 29 U.S.C. 623(f)(3).

[50] Johnson v. Minnesota Historical Society, 931 F.2d 1239 (8th Cir. 1991).

[51] Wilson v. Firestone Tire & Rubber Co., 932 F.2d 510 (6th Cir. 1991).

F. What Kind of Damages are Available to an Aggrieved Employee under the ADEA?

Unlike Title VII and the ADA, the ADEA does not allow for the same categories of damages. It allows for back pay, reinstatement, front pay and attorneys' fees.[52] It does not permit compensatory damages (beyond what is provided above) or punitive damages like Title VII and the ADA, but it does permit recovery for liquidated damages if the employee can prove a willful violation of the statute, whereas Title VII and the ADA do not allow for liquidated damages. Liquidated damages is defined as doubling the compensation the employee receives such as the doubled amount of back wages.[53] Willful is defined as "the employer either knew or showed reckless disregard for the matter of whether its conduct was prohibited."[54] The employer may defend against a claim for liquidated damages based upon its "good faith" belief that it was not violating the law.

---

[52] 29 U.S.C. 626(b).
[53] Id.
[54] McLaughlin v. Richland Shoe Co. 486 U.S. 128 (S.Ct. 1988).

V. EQUAL PAY ACT OF 1963

A. What is the Equal Pay Act?

The Equal Pay Act obligates employers to provide equal pay for men and women who perform "equal work", unless the difference in pay is based on seniority, merit system or some other factor other than sex. Men are protected under the EPA equally with women.

B. Does the Employee Have to Initially Pursue His/Her Claim with the Equal Employment Opportunity Commission (EEOC)?

Unlike Title VII, the ADEA and the ADA, an aggrieved employee is not required to initially process a claim under the EPA through the Equal Employment Opportunity Commission (EEOC).

C. What Employers are Covered by the EPA?

Any employer engaged in commerce or in the production of goods for commerce, which includes activities closely related or directly essential to the production of goods for commerce, is covered under the EPA.

D. How is Equal Work Defined?

Equal work under the EPA does not necessarily mean identical work. Work is "equal" if the job duties are "substantially equal".[55] The focus is on duties actually being performed not on title, motive or inaccurate job descriptions.

---

[55] Waters v. Turner, Wood & Smith Ins. Agency, 874 F.2d 797 (11th Cir. 1989).

"Equal work" is defined as jobs, the performance of which requires equal skill, effort, responsibility and which are performed under similar working conditions. All elements of the definition must be satisfied.

E. How are Wages Defined?

"Wages" is defined as all aspects of compensation as well as the value of "fringe benefits" such as health care benefits, vacations, and paid leave.[56]

Premium pay for overtime and hazardous duty are also considered wages and must be provided to male and female employees at the same rate.

F. When is an Employer Justified in Paying Men and Women at Different Rates?

There is no violation of the EPA to pay a male employee more than a female employee doing equal work if the difference is due to their relative length of service with the employer or to an objective evaluation system. The system must be uniformly applied to men and women and must have been imposed in good faith without the intention of avoiding compliance with the EPA.

An employer may justify the pay difference for equal work if the difference is based on any other factor other than sex. These factors may include the following:

a. Shift Differentials

Payment of a different rate for the time of day or the day of the week the work is performed. The standard must be uniformly applied and gender neutral.[57] For example, a male security guard gets paid more than a female security guard. The

---

[56] 29 CFR 1620.11.
[57] Corning Glass Works v. Brennan, 417 U.S. 188 (1974).

difference in pay is due to the male employee working the night shift; the female employee works the day shift. All night shift security guards get paid a higher hourly rate. The employer can justify paying the female employee a lower hourly rate under these circumstances. However, if the female security guard goes from day shift to night shift, she should be offered the same hourly rate as the male security guard.

b. Higher Education or More Experience

Compensation for education and experience can be reflected in wages. However, the education or experience receiving the premium must have some relationship to the job the employee is performing. It must also be uniformly applied pursuant to an objective, rational system.[58] For example, a male employee and a female employee are both computer programmers within the company. The employer can pay the male computer programmer a higher rate based upon him having a specialized degree in computer programming as compared to the female employee who does not have an advanced education in computer programming.

c. Salary Matching

To recruit new or experienced employees, an employer may match or exceed the salary earned elsewhere by the person being recruited. An employer may also match the bona fide offers made by other employers.[59] For example, a male employee informs his employer that he is leaving the company because he received an offer for another job that pays $10,000 more in salary compared to his salary at the company. The employer can offer to match the salary if the employee stays even if the male employee will be earning more than his female co-workers who hold the same position.

---

[58] <u>Wu v. Thomas</u>, 863 F.2d 1543 (11th Cir. 1989).
[59] <u>Winkes v. Brown Univ.</u>, 747 F.2d 792 (1st Cir. 1984); <u>Bazemore v. Friday</u>, 478 U.S. 385 (1986).

d. Profits

An employer may pay premium rates to an employee based on the profit attributable to the work of that employee.[60] For example, an employer can render a male sales employee a larger end of year bonus than a female sales employee if the bonus is based upon the male employee achieving higher sales for the company compared to the female sales employee.

G. What Damages are Available under the EPA?

In addition to the difference in salary between the two positions that require equal work, such as back pay, the aggrieved employee may also be reinstated, recover front pay for claims that involve retaliation when discharge is involved, attorneys' fees and liquidated damages (double recovery) such as an amount equal to the back wage liability. An employee cannot recover compensatory damages (other than what is provided above) or punitive damages. An employer may defeat the employee's claim for liquidated damages through a "good faith" defense concerning its belief that the difference in pay between the male and female worker was legal.

---

[60] Hodgson v. Kobert Hall Clothes, Inc., 473 F.2d 589 (3d Cir. 1973).

VI. FAMILY AND MEDICAL LEAVE ACT OF 1993

A. What is the Family and Medical Leave Act of 1993?

The Federal Family and Medical Leave Act of 1993 (FMLA) was passed to allow employees to attend to family and medical issues without having concern for job security. It allows employees to take a limited unpaid leave of absence under certain conditions. [61]

B. What Employers are Subject to the FMLA?

The statute applies to employers that employ fifty (50) or more employees during each 20 or more workweeks during the current or preceding year.[62] However, an employer should be mindful that even if the FMLA is not applicable, a circumstance requiring a leave of absence due to an employee's health condition may implicate the Americans with Disabilities Act (ADA) or state family and medical leave statutes. The ADA may require an employer to accommodate an employee by allowing an employee to take a leave of absence based upon a qualified disability recognized under the ADA.

C. Is the Leave Paid or Unpaid?

FMLA leave is unpaid however the employer can require that the employee apply any of his/her unused sick, vacation or personal time to the leave based upon the employer's policies regarding these benefits. For example, employee requires twelve (12) weeks of leave for employee's own serious health condition.[63] Employee has two (2) weeks of unused vacation time, three (3) sick days and two (2) personal days which employee has not used. The employer can requires that the employee apply this time to the

---

[61] 29 U.S.C. 2601 et seq.; 29 C.F.R. 825.100; 29 C.F.R. 825.101.
[62] 29 U.S.C. 2611(A); 29 C.F.R. 825.104.
[63] 29 C.F.R. 825.208.

FMLA leave so that the first three (3) weeks of the employees leave is paid and the remaining nine (9) weeks are unpaid. If the leave is for a family member with a serious health condition, the employer can require the employee to apply his three (3) sick days to the leave if the employer's sick leave policy allows the employee to use the sick days for an ill family member.

D. Does the Employee Accrue Benefits While on FMLA Leave?

The employer is responsible for maintaining the employee's health insurance as if the employee is actively working for the employer during the leave. The employee must pay any contribution or co-pays to the insurance as if actively working during the leave.[64] However, if the employee fails to return from the leave, the cost of the continued benefits during FMLA leave may be recouped by the employer unless the employee cannot return due to his/her serious health condition or based upon circumstances beyond the employee's control. [65]

E. How Does an Employee Qualify for FMLA Leave?

Employees who have worked for their employer for at least twelve (12) months and have worked at least 1,250 hours over the previous twelve (12) months, are eligible for unpaid, job-protected leave of up to twelve (12) weeks each year for family and medical reasons.[66]

F. Under What Circumstances is an FMLA Leave Permitted?

An unpaid leave may be taken for:

1. The birth of an employee's child and the care of the child (applicable to both mothers and fathers);

---

[64] 29 U.S.C. 2614.
[65] 29 U.S.C. 2614(c).
[66] 29 U.S.C. 2611(1).

2.   The placement of a child with the employee for adoption or foster care;

3.   The care of the employee's spouse, child or parent, who has a serious health condition; and

4.   A serious health condition that renders the employee unable to perform the functions of his/her job.[67]

G. How are the Terms Child, Parent and Serious Health Condition Defined under the FMLA?

A "child" includes biological, adopted, and foster child, step-child, legal ward or a "child" of a person acting in the capacity of a parent.[68]

The term "parent" includes biological parents, as well as a person that acted in the capacity of a parent toward the employee. Siblings and in-laws are not covered by the FMLA.[69] For example, an employee can take FMLA leave to care for a newborn child of his girlfriend even if the employee is not the biological father of the child. It is enough that the employee is to care for the newborn as if the child was the employee's child.

A "serious health condition" is defined as an illness, injury, impairment, or physical or mental condition that involves:

1.   Any period of incapacity or treatment connected with inpatient care (i.e., an overnight stay) in a hospital, hospice, or residential medical care facility; or

2.   A period of incapacity requiring absence of more than three calendar days from work, school, or other regular daily activities that also involves continuing treatment by (or under the supervision of) a health care provider; or

---

[67] 29 U.S.C. 2612(1).
[68] 29 C.F.R. 825.113.
[69] 29 C.F.R. 825.113.

3.   Any period of incapacity due to pregnancy, or for prenatal care; or

4.   Any period of incapacity (or treatment therefore) due to a chronic serious health condition (e.g., asthma, diabetes, epilepsy, etc.); or

5.   A period of incapacity that is permanent or long-term due to a condition for which treatment may not be effective (e.g., Alzheimer's, stroke, terminal disease, etc.); or

6.   Any absences to receive multiple treatments (including any period of recovery that follows) by, or on referral by, a health care provider for a condition that likely would result in incapacity of more than three consecutive days if left untreated (e.g., chemotherapy, physical therapy, dialysis, etc.).[70]

H. What if an Employee has More than One Qualifying Event?

An employee with more than one qualifying event within a twelve (12) month period is not entitled to a separate twelve (12) week period of leave for each event.[71] For example, if employee experiences a serious health condition and takes three (3) weeks of FMLA, the employee has nine (9) weeks left of FMLA leave should another FMLA qualifying event occur within the twelve (12) month period, such as to care for a spouse with a serious health condition.

I. Must the Employee Take the Twelve (12) Weeks of Leave All at Once?

---

[70] 29 C.F.R. 825.114; www.dol.gov, Family and Medical Leave Advisor, definition of "serious health condition".

[71] 29 C.F.R. 825.200.

The leave does not need to be taken all at one time. Intermittent leave or reduced leave (less than 12 weeks) can be taken if the employee or a covered relation has a serious health condition, provided intermittent or reduced leave is medically necessary. Intermittent leave is taken by the hour, day or week.[72] Reduced leave allows the employee to work fewer hours per week or per day.[73] Intermittent and reduced leave is not available for healthy births or adoptions unless the employer agrees.[74] For example, employee takes six (6) weeks of leave to care for the birth of her newborn. Employee wishes to take remaining six (6) weeks on a part-time basis, working 9:00 a.m. to 1:00 p.m., Monday through Friday. The employer can deny the leave request. The six (6) weeks of leave taken on a part-time basis is considered reduced leave and is being requested to care for a healthy child. Reduced leave is not available to care for a healthy newborn. If the child had a serious health condition, the employer could not deny the request for reduced leave.

J.   What Responsibilities Does the Employee Have with FMLA Leave?

It is up to the employer to determine if an employee's absence or request to be absent qualifies as FMLA leave. The employee does not have to request that he/she be permitted the leave under FMLA. The employer must designate leave as FMLA leave and give notice to the employee. [75] The employer's designation of the absence as FMLA leave must be made before the leave starts unless the employer does not have sufficient information as to the employee's reason for taking the leave. If the employer does not designate an employee's absence as FMLA leave, the leave taken does not count against the employee's FMLA leave entitlement. [76]

However, the U.S. Supreme Court ruled in Ragsdale v. Wolverine World Wide, Inc. that 29 C.F.R. 825.700(a) that the requirement to designate leave as FMLA leave is invalid. The employee in the case was granted seven (7)

---

[72] 29 C.F.R. 825.203(b).
[73] 29 C.F.R. 825.203(c).
[74] 29 U.S.C. 2611 (a); 29 U.S.C. 2611 (b).
[75] 29 C.F.R. 208.
[76] 29 C.F.R. 825.700(a).

months (30 weeks) of leave under the company's policy, more than the twelve (12) week leave entitlement under the FMLA. However, the employer did not designate the leave as FMLA leave. At the end of the 30 weeks, the employee was not able to return to work and requested twelve (12) more weeks of leave under FMLA. The employer refused the request and terminated the employee. The Court determined that the regulation is invalid because it imposes a "categorical penalty on employers" by forcing them to provide up to twelve (12) additional weeks of leave if the employer does not provide proper notice under FMLA.

However, it is the employee's responsibility to provide a medical certification from a healthcare provider. The certification certifies the serious health condition of the employee or the employee's parent, spouse or child with a serious health condition, who the employee will care for while on FMLA leave. The employer can require that the healthcare certification provide the following information:

1. Date the condition began;
2. Probable duration;
3. Medical facts regarding the condition;
4. If leave is sought for care giving, a statement that the employee is needed to give care and the amount of time needed;
5. If leave is sought for the employee's own serious health condition, a statement that the employee is unable to perform the functions of his/her position;
6. If the leave is sought on an intermittent or reduced basis, a statement that such leave is necessary and the expected duration.[77]

The FMLA regulations also provide that if the leave is foreseeable, the employee is required to provide at least 30 days notice prior to the leave beginning. If the leave needs to begin in less than 30 days, the employee must provide such notice as is practicable.

---

[77] 29 U.S.C. 2613.

K. How Does an Employer Compute the Twelve-Month Period for Purposes of FMLA?

Four methods are available to compute the 12-month period to determine how many weeks are available to an employee at a given time. The employer can use the calendar year, any fixed twelve-month period, the 12-month period measured forward or the rolling method.[78]

Under the calendar year approach the period of entitlement lasts through the year and is renewed on January 1st of each year.

If the employer chooses to use a different fixed twelve-month period such as an employee's anniversary date of hire. This anniversary date can serve as the start date and end date for the FMLA period.

The 12-moth period measured forward is calculated from the date the employee first takes FMLA leave. The next 12-month period would begin the first time the FMLA leave is taken after completion of any previous 12-month period. For example, employee takes 12 weeks of leave beginning May 7, 2007. Her leave would therefore run from May 1, 2007 to April 31, 2008. In future years the employee's leave would run again when the employee needs leave.

The rolling method uses a 12-month period measured backward from the date on which an employee uses any FMLA leave. The employee's leave entitlement is equal to any unused part of the twelve-week leave not used in the immediately preceding twelve-month period. The immediately preceding twelve-month period provides a window which changes daily. For example, employee uses two (2) weeks of FMLA leave in September 2007 (September 3, 2007 to September 14, 2007), another two (2) weeks in November 2007 (November 12, 2007 to November 23, 2007), and an additional two (2) weeks in December 2007 (December 10, 2007 to December 21, 2007). Employee asks employer on September 1, 2008 how much entitlement time she has left. To calculate that amount under the rolling method, the employer would look back 12 months to September 1, 2007 and count up the total FMLA leave the employee used to determine how much time is remaining. Hence, from September 1, 2007 to September 1, 2008, the employee has used six (6) weeks of FMLA leave, therefore she has six (6) weeks of FMLA leave remaining.

---

[78] 29 C.F.R. 825.200(b).

If the employee asks about her remaining FMLA time on October 27, 2008, looking back at the immediately preceding 12 months, the two (2) weeks that the employee took from September 3, 2007 to September 14, 2007 are no longer in the 12 month window, therefore the employee has only used four (4) weeks of FMLA leave with eight (8) weeks of FMLA leave remaining for her use.

The rolling method only includes those weeks of leave that were used in the applicable window of the previous twelve (12) months; any leave used prior to that time is not included in the calculation.

Employers are attracted to the rolling method because it eliminates the "stacking" of FMLA time, which can arise under the other three (3) methods. For example, under the calendar year approach, an employee can take the last twelve (12) weeks of 2007 as FMLA and the first twelve (12) weeks of 2008 as FMLA leave therefore remaining out on leave for 24 weeks or six (6) months since the employee is eligible for twelve (12) weeks of leave January 1 of each year. The rolling method protects employers from stacking, although it is a more complex approach compared to the other methods available.

L. How is FMLA Applied when there is Also a State Statute that Governs Family and Medical Leaves?

Many states have also enacted their own laws that govern leaves of absences under qualifying conditions that are the same as the FMLA or expand upon the FMLA qualifying events. The FMLA provides that the Act does not supersede any state or local law which provides greater rights than those established by the FMLA.[79] If an occurrence qualifies under the FMLA and a state statute, the leave may run concurrently under both statutes. If the state statute allows leave for a situation that does not qualify under the FMLA, then only the requirements of the state statute is controlling and the employee would have FMLA available to use at a later date should a qualifying event arise. In sum, an employer must comply with both the FMLA and state statutes that provide family and medical leave.

---

[79] 29 U.S.C. 2651(b).

M. Can FMLA Apply When an Employee Experiences a Workers' Compensation Injury?

State workers' compensation laws are designed to provide benefits to injured employees, regardless of fault, for a work related accident or illness. Even if an employee was totally negligent in causing his injury, the employer had been totally at fault, or both parties were responsible, full coverage is afforded with no deduction for comparative fault of the employee. Fault is not an issue for coverage. Coverage can include injury sustained during paid lunch hours and away from the work place if there exists some nexus between the work and the circumstances in which the employee is injured. It may also include injury sustained at a company holiday party, when on-call as well as other situations.

A work related injury that prevents an employee from performing the functions of his/her job can qualify as a serious health condition under the FMLA and also trigger benefits under workers' compensation laws. If so, the employer is not permitted to require the employee to use paid vacation or any other paid leave if the worker receives workers' compensation benefits.

In the event that an employee has a serious illness that qualifies as FMLA leave and entitles the employee to benefits under workers' compensation, the employer may require the twelve (12) week FMLA leave to run concurrently with any leave permitted under workers' compensation.

VII. THE FAIR LABOR STANDARDS ACT (FLSA)

The Fair Labor Standard Act (FLSA) was passed to set minimum wage, overtime pay, equal pay (pursuant to the Equal Pay Act) and record keeping requirements for workers. It also governs child labor issues.

Under the FLSA there is an important distinction between those employees who are subject to the FLSA and those employees who are exempt from the FLSA. This chapter will focus on the overtime provisions of the FLSA. If an employee is exempt from the FLSA the employer is not required to pay the employee overtime. Employees who are exempt from the FLSA are referred to as the "white collar exemptions". These employees usually fall into the categories of executive, administrative and professional employees. Outside salespersons are also exempt from the FLSA.[80] On April 23, 2004 the U.S. Department of Labor (DOL) made a number of changes that were intended to clarify and simplify exempt status under the FLSA. These changes went into effect on August 23, 2004. The changes concern the additional exempt categories of the computer professional and the highly compensated employee.

A. How Does the FLSA Define Employer?

The FLSA defines employer to include "any person acting directly or indirectly in the interest of an employer in relation to an employee".[81] The courts broadly interpret this definition.

B. Who Enforces the FLSA?

The FLSA is enforced by the Wage and Hour Division within the DOL.

Although the FLSA is a federal statute, it does not preempt state statutes that govern wage and hour issues. As such, an employer is required to be in

---

[80] 29 C.F.R. 541.500.
[81] 29 U.S.C. 203(d).

compliance with both the FLSA and any state statutes that address the same issues as the FLSA.[82]

C. When is an Employee Entitled to Overtime?

An employer is required to pay employees who are nonexempt, overtime pay for every hour worked over 40 in a week. Overtime is defined as one and one-half times the employee's hourly rate. Overtime is not required based upon daily hours, when an employee works on a holiday or when an employee works on the weekend. For example, if an employee works four, ten hour days in a given week, he/she is not entitled to overtime because at the end of the week the employee has only worked 40 hours. Moreover, an employer is not required to pay an employee overtime for hours worked on a Saturday, if at the end of the week the employee only works 40 hours. Finally, if an employee works on July 4th (assuming it falls on a Monday) and works only 40 hours for the remainder of the week, the employee is not entitled to overtime. Although the FLSA sets minimum requirements for overtime, an employer may pay overtime to employees even though such overtime is not required under FLSA. For example, an employer may pay an employee overtime for any hour worked over eight hours in a day; for work on a holiday; or work on a weekend.

D. How Does an Employer Determine Exempt Status?

In order to determine whether an employee is exempt from the FLSA it is crucial that the employee's job responsibilities are analyzed pursuant to the white collar exemptions. It is not enough that the employer gives an employee a title that appears to fall under one of the exemptions. The employee's job responsibilities are controlling. For example, an employer cannot rest its determination that an administrative assistant is an exempt administrative employee simply by the employee's title. The employee's job responsibilities are what control in determining exempt status.

In addition, the employee must be paid on a salary basis as compared to an hourly basis. That is, the employee must receive each pay period a predetermined amount that is not subject to reduction based on the quality or quantity of work performed. In addition, there is generally a salary threshold.

---

[82] See, 29 U.S.C. 218.

The minimum salary level for the exempt worker is $23,660 a year or $455 per week.[83] However, this salary requirement does not apply to the outside sales employee exemption.[84] In addition, the computer employee may meet the compensation requirement on an hourly basis at a rate not less than $27.63 an hour.[85]

E. How Does the FLSA Define an Exempt Administrative Employee?

Under the FLSA, an employee is an exempt administrative employee if the employee has the following characteristics:

1. The employee is compensated on a salary or fee basis (as defined in the regulations) at a rate not less than $455 per week;

2. Has the primary duty of office or non-manual work directly related to the management or general business operations of the employer or the employer's customers; and

3. Exercises discretion and independent judgment with respect to matters of significance.[86]

F. What is Meant by the "Primary Duty of Exempt Work" for the Administrative Employee?

The exempt administrator must perform "primary duty" of exempt work. Primary duty is defined as "the principle, main, major or most important duty that the employee performs". The amount of time spent doing exempt work can be helpful in determining an employee's primary duty. As a general "rule of thumb" an employee who spends more than 50% of his/her time performing exempt work will satisfy the primary duty factor.[87]

---

[83] 29 C.F.R. 541.602.
[84] 29 C.F.R. 541.500 (c).
[85] 29 C.F.R. 541.600(d); 29 C.F.R. 541.400(b).
[86] 29 C.F.R. 541.200.
[87] 29 C.F.R. 541.700.

G. What is Meant by "Directly Related to Management or General Business Operations" as Required by the Administrative Exemption?

"Directly related to management or general business operations" requires that the employee perform work directly related to assisting with the running or servicing of the business, as compared to working on a manufacturing production line or selling a product in a retail or service establishment.[88]

H. What is Meant by the "Exercise of Discretion and Independent Judgment" as Required by the Administrative Exemption?

The "discretion and independent judgment" factor involves the comparison and the evaluation of possible courses of conduct and acting or making a decision after considering the various possibilities. All the facts involved in the employee's particular employment situation are evaluated. The employee is to have the ability to make an independent choice, unbound by immediate direction or supervision. This is not to say that the employee's decisions cannot be revised or reversed after reviewed by a "higher level". The decision can consist of recommended action. [89]

Factors to consider when evaluating discretion and independent judgment include the following:

- whether the employee has authority to formulate, affect, interpret, or implement management policies or operating practices;

- whether the employee carries out major assignments in conducting the operations of the business;

---

[88] 29 C.F.R. 541.201.
[89] 29 C.F.R. 541.202.

- whether the employee performs work that affects business operations to a substantial degree;

- whether the employee has authority to commit the employer in matters that have significant financial impact;

- whether the employee has authority to waive or deviate from established policies and procedures without prior approval. [90]

I. What are Some Examples of Positions that May Qualify under the Administrative Exemption?

While the responsibilities of the position concerning the administrative exemption characteristics controls, the following are some positions that may qualify as exempt administrative employees under the FLSA: insurance claim adjuster, executive and administrative assistants, purchasing agent and human resources manager.

J. How Does the FLSA Define an Exempt Professional Employee?

Under the changes to the FLSA, the duties test for an exempt professional employee has been clarified. The duties vary whether the employee is being defined as a learned professional or a creative professional.

K. What is a Learned Professional?

A learned professional employee's primary duty is the performance of work requiring advanced knowledge, defined as work which is predominantly intellectual in character and which includes work requiring the consistent exercise of discretion and judgment.[91]

---

[90] 29 C.F.R. 541.202(b).
[91] 29 C.F.R. 541.301.

In addition to the employee's primary duty described above, the learned professional employee exemption also has the following characteristics:

1.   The employee must be compensated on a salary or fee basis at a rate not less than $455 per week;

2.   The advanced knowledge must be in a field of science or learning; and

3.   The advanced knowledge must be customarily acquired by a prolonged course of specialized intellectual instruction.[92]

L. What is Meant by the Requirement of "Advanced Knowledge" for the Learned Professional Exemption?

Advanced knowledge "must customarily be acquired by a prolonged course of specialized intellectual study".[93] The work must be predominantly intellectual in character and includes the "consistent exercise of discretion and independent judgment as compared to routine mental, manual, mechanical or physical work". It cannot be attained at the high school level. [94]

M. What is Meant by the Requirement of Possessing Advanced Knowledge in a "Field of Science or Learning" for the Learned Professional Exemption?

A field of science or learning includes such areas "that have a recognized professional status" such as law, medicine, theology, accounting, actuarial computation, engineering, architecture, teaching, various types of physical, chemical and biological sciences, pharmacy and other similar professional occupations. Mechanical arts or skilled trades do not satisfy this factor although knowledge in such fields could be fairly advanced.[95]

---

[92] Id.
[93] 29 C.F.R. 541.301(a)(3).
[94] 29 C.F.R. 541.301(b).
[95] 29 C.F.R. 541.301(c).

N. What is Meant by the Requirement of a "Prolonged Course of Specialized Intellectual Instruction" for the Learned Professional Exemption?

The learned professional exemption is restricted to "professions where specialized academic training is a standard prerequisite for entrance into the profession. The best evidence of meeting this requirement is having the appropriate academic degree". This exemption "does not apply to occupations in which most employees acquire their skill by experience rather than by advanced specialized intellectual instruction.".[96]

Examples of professions that generally meet the duties requirement of the learned professional exemption are as follows: registered or certified medical technologists; registered nurses; dental hygienists; physician assistants; accountants; executive chefs and sous chefs; paralegal who also possess advanced specialized degrees in other professional fields (i.e., a paralegal who has an engineering degree and draws on that experience to advise on product liability cases); athletic trainers; and, funeral directors and embalmers. However, under each profession described, the DOL is clear on required academic study and accreditation.[97]

O. What is a Creative Professional?

A creative professional employee's primary duty is the performance of work requiring invention, imagination, originality or talent in a recognized field of artistic or creative endeavor.[98]

In addition to the employee's primary duty described above, the learned professional also must be compensated on a salary or fee basis at a rate not less than $455 per week.

---

[96] 29 C.F.R. 541.301(c).
[97] 29 C.F.R. 541.301(e).
[98] 29 C.F.R. 541.302(a).

P. What is Meant by the Requirement of Requiring "Invention, Imagination, Originality or Talent" for the Creative Professional Exemption?

This creative professional employee's work does not depend on intelligence, diligence and accuracy but rather invention, imagination, originality or talent exercised by the employee. Application of the exemption is fact sensitive. The requirements are "generally met by actors, musicians, composers, soloists, certain painters, writers, cartoonists, essayists and novelists". The employee is provided a title or underlying concept and the creative professional utilizes his/her "creative ability to express the concept".[99] The fact-sensitive application of the exemption can be appreciated with journalists. The duties requirement for a journalist as a creative professional employee, applies if the employee's primary duty is work requiring invention, imagination, originality or talent. The same profession would not meet creative professional exemption if the employee only collects, organizes and records information that is routine or already public, or if they do not contribute a unique interpretation or analysis to a news product.[100]

Q. How Does the FLSA Define an Exempt Executive Employee?

Under the FLSA, an employee is an exempt executive employee if the employee has the following characteristics:

1. The employee must be compensated on a salary basis at a rate not less than $455 per week;

2. Has the primary duty of managing the enterprise, or managing a customarily recognized department or subdivision of the enterprise;

3. Customarily and regularly directs the work of at least two or more other full-time employees or their equivalent; and

4. Has the authority to hire or fire other employees, or the employee's

---

[99] 29 C.F.R. 541.302(c).
[100] 29 C.F.R. 541.302(d).

suggestions and recommendations as to the hiring, firing, advancement, promotion or any other change of status of other employees must be given particular weight.[101]

R. What is Meant by the "Primary Duty of Managing" Under the Executive Employee Exemption?

Primary duty is defined as the "main, major or most important duty", which is determined by looking at the employee's job duties as a whole.[102] The exempt executive employee must have the primary duty of managing, which includes such activities as:

- interviewing, selecting, and training employees;
- setting and adjusting their rates of pay and work hours;
- planning and directing the work of other employees;
- maintaining sales or production records;
- appraising employees' productivity and efficiency for recommending promotions or other changes in status;
- handling employee complaints and grievances;
- disciplining employees;
- determining the techniques to be used;
- apportioning work among the employees;
- determining the type of materials, supplies, machinery, equipment or tools to be used or merchandise to be bought, stocked and sold;
- providing safety and security of the employees or property;
- planning and controlling the budget;
- monitoring or implementing legal compliance measures.[103]

S. What is Meant by a "Recognized Department or Subdivision of the Enterprise" Under the Executive Employee Exemption?

A "recognized department or subdivision" was inserted as one of the characteristics of the executive employee exemption to distinguish between a

---

[101] 29 C.F.R. 541.100.
[102] 29 C.F.R. 541.700.
[103] 29 C.F.R. 541.102.

collection of employees who are assigned from time to time to a specific job or series of jobs as compared to a unit with permanent status and function such as a human resources department, which is of a permanent nature and would qualify as a recognized department. The following subdivisions of a human resources department would also qualify as recognized subdivisions under the definition due to their permanency in nature: labor relations, equal employment, pension and benefits.[104]

T. Are there any Special Characteristics of the Two or More Employees Requirement of the Executive Employee Exemption?

The phrase "two or more employees" requires the employees to be full-time or their equivalent. As such, one full-time employee and two part-time employees or four part-time employees would meet the definition.[105]

U. What is Meant by the Exempt Executive Employee's Authority as to Employee Status Having "Particular Weight" Under the Executive Employee Exemption?

The purpose of the characteristic of the exempt executive employee's authority having particular weight is intended to distinguish from occasional suggestions made by the exempt executive, which is not sufficient to meet the definition of an exempt executive employee. Factors that can be considered in determining whether an exempt executive's recommendations are given particular weight include: whether it is part of the executive's job to make such recommendations; and the frequency in which such requests are made, requested and relied upon. The executive's suggestions and recommendations can nevertheless have particular weight even if a higher level manager's determination has greater weight or if the executive does not make the final determination as to the employee's status. Proof of required authority can be determined from the executive's job description or performance reviews that demonstrate that the executive is involved in the promotion or other change in status of employees.[106]

---

[104] 29 C.F.R. 541.103.
[105] 29 C.F.R. 541.104.
[106] 29 C.F.R. 541.105.

V. Can Business Owners Qualify Under the Employee Executive Exemption ?

A private sector owner who has a 20 percent equity interest in a business in which he/she is employed is considered an exempt executive employee if the executive is engaged in the management of the business without having to meet the salary basis test. [107]

W. What are Examples of Positions that May Qualify Under the Executive Exemption?

While it is the responsibilities of the position as it relates to the executive exemption characteristics that controls, the following are some positions that may qualify as exempt executive employees under the FLSA: senor merchandizing manager, production supervisor, store manager and EMS director.

X. How Does the FLSA Define an Exempt Outside Sales Employee?

Under the FLSA, an employee is an exempt outside sales employee if the employee has the following characteristics:

1. Primary duty is to make sales or obtain orders or contracts for services or for the use of facilities for which a consideration will be paid by the client or customer; and

2. The employee is customarily and regularly engaged away from the employer's place or places of business.[108]

---

[107] 29 C.F.R. 541.101.
[108] 29 C.F.R. 541.500.

Y. What is Meant by "Away from the Employer's Place of Business" Under the Outside Sales Employee Exemption?

The outside sales employee makes sales at the customer's place of business, or, if selling door-to-door, at the customer's home. Outside sales does not include sales made by mail, telephone or the internet unless such contact is used with personal calls. Any fixed site, whether home or office, used by a salesperson as a headquarters or to solicit customers by telephone for the purpose of making sales is considered one of the employer's places of business, even if the employer is not the owner or tenant of the property.[109]

Z. How Does Promotional Work Effect an Outside Sales Employee's Exempt Status?

Promotional work, work that salespeople do to promote their product, is often part of any sales job. Promotional work that helps an outside sales person make his/her own sale is exempt work. However, promotional work designed to help someone else make sales is not exempt work. For example, an employee who visits store customers and assembles displays and removes or rearranges stock on customer shelves would qualify as an exempt outside sales employee as long as his/her primary duty is making sales or contracts. In contrast, an employee who does the same concerning removing and rearranging stock and customer shelves as described above, but leaves a product order form with the store manager to send in at a later date does not qualify as an exempt outside sales employee. This employee is not involved in consummating the sale, the primary duty of the exempt outside sales employee. [110]

AA. Can an Employee Engaged in Both Sales and Delivery be Considered an Exempt Outside Salesperson?

Drivers who deliver products and also sell such products may qualify as exempt outside sales employees only if the employee has a primary duty of

---

[109] 29 C.F.R. 541.502.
[110] 29 C.F.R. 541.503.

making sales.   Factors to consider in determining whether a driver has a primary duty of making sales include the following:

- The driver's duties compared with other employees who are drivers and salespersons;
- Whether there are customary or contractual arrangements concerning amounts of products to be delivered;
- Whether or not the driver has a selling or solicitor's license when required by law;
- The description of the employee's occupation in collective bargaining agreements;
- The specifications and requirements for the position;
- Whether the employee had sales training;
- Whether the driver attends sales conferences;
- How wages are paid to the driver;
- How much of the driver's wages are in connection with sales made.[111]

BB.   How Does the FLSA Define an Exempt Computer Employee?

Under the FLSA, an employee is and exempt computer employee if the employee has the following characteristics:

- The employee must be compensated either on a salary or fee basis of no less than $455 per week or, if compensated on an hourly basis, no less than $27.63 an hour;

- The employee must be employed as a computer systems analyst, computer programmer, software engineer or other similarly skilled worker in the computer field with his/her primary duty consisting of one of the following:

    1.   The application of systems analysis techniques and procedures, including consulting with users to determine hardware, software or system functional specifications;

---

[111] 29 C.F.R. 541.504.

2.   The design, development, documentation, analysis, creation, testing or modification of computer systems or programs, including prototypes, based on and related to user or system design specifications;

3.   The design, documentation, testing, creation or modification of computer programs related to machine operating systems; or

4.   A combination of the aforementioned duties, the performance of which requires the same level of skills.[112]

The computer employee exemption does not include employees engaged in the manufacture or repair of computer hardware and related equipment.[113]

CC. What are Examples of Jobs that May Qualify Under the Computer Employee Exemption?

While it is the responsibilities of the position as it relates to the computer employee exemption characteristics that controls, the following are some positions that may qualify as exempt executive employees under the FLSA: analysts, programmers and engineers.

DD. How Does the FLSA Define the Highly Compensated Exempt Employee?

The FLSA regulations have included a special rule for "highly-compensated" workers who are paid total annual compensation of $100,000 or more. Such employees are exempt under the FLSA if the employee has the following characteristics:

1.   The employee earns total annual compensation of $100,000 or more, which includes at least $455 per week paid on a salary basis;

---

[112] 29 C.F.R. 541.400.
[113] 29 C.F.R. 541.401.

2. The employee's primary duty includes performing office or non-manual work; and

3. The employee customarily and regularly performs at least one of the exempt duties or responsibilities of an exempt executive, administrative or professional employee.[114]

By this definition, an employee can qualify as an exempt highly-compensated executive if the employee customarily and regularly directs the work of two or more other employees, even if the employee does not meet all of the other requirements in the standard test for the executive exemption. Alternatively, he/she would also qualify under the third criteria in connection with the executive exemption if he/she had the authority to hire or fire or make recommendations regarding hire or fire that are given particular weight.[115]

To fulfill the third characteristic under the administrative exemption the employee would need to perform office or non-manual work directly related to the management or general business operations of the employer or the employer's customers; or, exercises discretion and independent judgment with respect to matters of significance. [116]

Similarly, as to the professional exemption, the employee would need to perform work requiring knowledge of an advanced nature in a field of science or learning customarily acquired through a prolonged course of specialized instruction; or requiring invention, imagination, originality or talent in a recognized field of artistic or creative endeavor.[117]

EE. How is the $100,000 Compensation Figure Calculated for the Highly Compensated Exempt Employee?

The required total annual compensation of at least $100,000 may consist of commissions, nondiscretionary bonuses and other nondiscretionary compensation earned during a 52-week period. It does not include credit for

---

[114] 29 C.F.R. 541.601.
[115] 29 C.F.R. 541.100.
[116] 29 C.F.R. 541.200.
[117] 29 C.F.R. 541.301; 29 C.F.R. 541.302(a).

board or lodging, payments for medical or life insurance, or contributions to retirement plans or other fringe benefits.[118]

FF. What Happens if an Employee Only Works Part of the Year or Does Not Meet the $100,000 Threshold at the End of the Year?

If an employee does not work the full year for an employer either because of his/her hire date or if he employee's employment ends prior to the end of the year, the employee may nevertheless qualify for the highly compensated employee exemption if he/she received a pro rata portion of the $100,000 threshold based upon the number of weeks the employee will be or has been employed.[119]

If the employee's total annual income does not meet the $100,000 threshold by the end of the year, the employer will have one month to make one final payment sufficient to meet the required level of compensation. If the employer fails to make the payment, the employee does not qualify under the highly compensated exemption. However, he/she may nevertheless qualify as exempt under the administrative, executive or professional exemptions depending upon the employee's job responsibilities.[120]

GG. Which Occupations are Specifically Excluded from the Highly Compensated Employee Exemption?

The FLSA Regulations specifically provide that the highly compensated employee exemption applies to employees who perform office or non-manual work. As such, irrespective of income, the highly compensated exemption would not apply to such professions as carpenters, electricians, mechanics, plumbers, iron workers, craftsmen, operating engineers, longshoremen, construction workers and laborers.[121]

---

[118] 29 C.F.R. 541.601.
[119] Id.
[120] Id.
[121] Id.

HH. What are Considered Improper Deductions from an Exempt Employee's Salary, which can Jeopardize His/Her Exempt Status?

If an employer makes improper deductions from an exempt employee's pay, the employer can jeopardize the employee's exempt status. In general, one of the elements of an exempt employee is that the employee is paid a salary of at least $455 per week irrespective of quality or quantity of work. For example, if an exempt employee has an attendance problem, the employee should not be suspended with his salary docketed as a form of discipline in response to the attendance issue. Similarly, an exempt employee's salary cannot be affected by absences due to jury duty, attendance as a witness or temporary military leave. However, an employer can offset any amounts received by the employee as jury or witness fees or military pay.[122] An employer should avoid jeopardizing an employee's exempt status under the FLSA otherwise the employee will be considered non-exempt and the employer will be required to follow all FLSA requirements for the employee including record keeping requirements and overtime pay. In addition the employer will be exposed to lawsuit and penalties by the DOL.

II. What is the "Safe Harbor" Rule?

If an employer makes impermissible deductions from an exempt employee's status, the employee's exempt status will not be lost if the deductions are "isolated" or "inadvertent" and if the employee is reimbursed. This is referred to as the "safe harbor" rule. The employer must demonstrate a good faith effort to comply with the FLSA by:

- having a clearly communicated policy prohibiting improper deductions, including a complaint mechanism,

- reimbursing the employee for any improper deductions, and

- making a good faith commitment to comply in the future.

---

[122] 29 C.F.R. 541.602.

However, the employer will lose the "safe harbor" if it willfully violates the policy by continuing the improper deductions after receiving employee complaints.[123]

JJ. When are Deductions Permissible for Exempt Employees Under the FLSA?

Employers are permitted to dock exempt employees' wages on a day-by-day basis for violation of "workplace conduct" rules if the rules are outlined in a written policy. Examples of such inappropriate or illegal conduct that would be embodied in workplace conduct rules include sexual harassment, workplace violence, drug and alcohol use or violations of state and federal laws. Employers may also make workday deductions, in increments of a full day, for safety rules of major significance. An example of violating a safety rule of major significance would be smoking in explosive plants, oil refineries or coal mines.[124]

Employers can charge an employee's leave bank on a partial-day absences such as to go to the dentist. For example, the employer can charge three hours for the appointment to the employee's vacation time or sick leave without interfering with the employee's exempt status.[125]

---

[123] 29 C.F.R. 541.603.
[124] 29 C.F.R. 541.602.
[125] 29 C.F.R. 541.602.

INDEX

A

B

C

D

E

Labor Law
SPARK LAW SERIES

Labor Law
SPARK LAW SERIES

Labor Law
SPARK LAW SERIES

Notes

Notes

Notes

Notes

Notes

Notes

Notes

Notes

Notes

Notes

Notes

Notes

Notes

Notes

Notes

Notes

Notes

Notes

Notes

Notes

Notes

Notes

Notes

Notes

Notes

Notes

Notes

Notes

Notes

Notes

Notes

Notes

Notes

Notes

Notes

Notes

Notes

Notes

Notes

Notes

Notes

Notes

Notes

Notes

Notes

Notes

Notes

Notes

Notes

Notes

Notes

Notes

Notes

Notes

Notes

Notes

Notes

Notes

Notes

Notes

Notes

Notes

Notes

Notes

Notes

Notes

Notes

Notes

Notes

Notes

Notes

Notes

Notes

Notes

Notes

Notes

Notes

Notes

Notes

Labor Law
SPARK LAW SERIES

Notes

Notes

Notes

Notes

Notes

Notes

Notes

Notes

Notes

Notes

Notes

Notes

Notes

Notes

Notes

Notes

Notes

Notes

Notes

Notes

Notes

Notes

Notes

Notes

Notes

Notes

Notes

Notes

Notes

Notes

Notes

Notes

Notes

Notes

Notes

Notes

Notes

Notes

Notes

Notes

Notes

Notes

Notes

Notes

Notes

Notes

Notes

Notes

Notes

Notes

Notes

Notes

Notes